See the puddles raindrops make.

See the ocean from the shore.

See the waves and hear them roar.

Water flows from sky to sea,
bringing life to you and me.

Water helps us all to grow –
every living thing we know.

We save water from the drains . . .

. . . and put out pans each time it rains.

We water all our plants and flowers,
with the water saved from showers.

Every morning, every night,
   we turn the tap off, good and tight!

We keep water fresh and clean.
Every river. Every stream.

We drink. We wash.
We work. We play.

We use water every day!

Creative Tot Time

Watering Can Craft

Children love working and playing with water. Including them in the household chore of watering plants in and around the house gives them a rewarding responsibility disguised as a whole lot of fun. With this recycled craft project, your tot will create his or her very own watering can. Best of all, carrying the water to and fro will give their large muscles a great workout, too!

What you need:

- A plastic milk carton, washed and rinsed
- Items to decorate your carton,
  such as paint and brushes
  or stickers
- Clear acrylic spray
- Nail and hammer

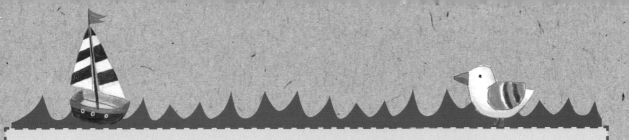

What you do:

1. Prepare your clean milk carton by removing any stickers.

2. Ask your child to decorate the carton by painting it and/or applying stickers. This is their masterpiece! Let it dry.

3. When the carton is dry, spray it with clear acrylic paint.

4. Using the nail and hammer, poke holes in the lid.

5. Help your child partially fill the carton with water. (It may become too heavy if filled all the way.) Your child can then put the lid on. Be sure to double-check that it is tight. Your carton is now ready to give your plants a drink!

For Charlotte and Christopher — CG

Raintree is an imprint of Capstone Global Library Limited, a company incorporated in England and Wales having its registered office at 7 Pilgrim Street, London, EC4V 6LB – Registered company number: 6695582

To contact Raintree:
Phone: 0845 6044371
Fax: + 44 (0) 1865 312263
Email: myorders@raintreepublishers.co.uk.
Customers from outside the UK please telephone +44 1865 312262.

Text © Charles Ghigna 2012
Illustrations © Picture Window Books 2012
First published in the UK in 2014
The moral rights of the proprietor have been asserted.

Designer: Joanna Hinton-Malivoire
Editor: Helen Cox Cannons
Production: Vicki Fitzgerald
Printed in China by Leo Paper Products Ltd

ISBN 978 1 406 26639 9
17 16 15 14 13
10 9 8 7 6 5 4 3 2 1

British Library Cataloguing in Publication Data
A full catalogue record for this book is available from the British Library.